CONCHIES

CONSCIENTIOUS OBJECTORS OF THE FIRST WORLD WAR

CONCHIES

CONSCIENTIOUS OBJECTORS
OF THE FIRST
WORLD WAR

ANN KRAMER

FRANKLIN WATTS
LONDON•SYDNEY

This edition published in 2014 by Franklin Watts

Copyright © Franklin Watts 2014

Franklin Watts
338 Euston Road
London NW1 3BH

Franklin Watts Australia
Level 17/207 Kent Street
Sydney, NSW 2000

A CIP catalogue record for this book is available from the British Library.

Dewey no: 940.3

Paperback ISBN: 978 1 4451 2640 1

Printed in the United Kingdom by Clays

Franklin Watts is a division of Hachette Children's Books, an Hachette UK company.

www.hachette.co.uk

Editor: Sarah Ridley
Editor in chief: John C. Miles
Designer: Jason Billin
Art director: Peter Scoulding
Picture research: Diana Morris

Picture credits:
Cover – PPU.

Kitchener – Wikimedia Commons; Keir Hardie – Stapleton Historical Collection/
HIP/Topfoto; 'The Conscientious Objector at the Front' – Courtesy of Tony Allen.
http://www.worldwar1postcards.com; 'What did you do in the Great War, Daddy?'
– World History Archive/Topfoto; Fenner Brockway, NCF Manifesto, COs in the
news – PPU; Tribunals cartoon, Coded postcard – Courtesy of Tony Allen. http://
www.worldwar1postcards.com; Field punishment – Photogenes; The 'Frenchmen',
Winchester Whisperer, Dyce work camp – PPU; Dartmoor – Picturepoint Topham;
CO plaque – PPU; CO memorial; John C. Miles.

CONTENTS

TIMETABLE TO WAR

1914

28 June: Serbian nationalist assassinates Archduke Franz Ferdinand, heir to the Austrian throne

28 July: Austria-Hungary declares war on Serbia

1 August: Germany declares war on Russia

3 August: Germany declares war on France

4 August: German troops enter Belgium

4 August: Britain declares war on Germany.

4 August: The First World War begins

INTRODUCTION

During the First World War (1914–18) millions of men left home to fight. They were told it was their duty to defend their country. But as the war progressed some men refused to fight because they believed it was wrong to kill. They were called conscientious objectors (COs), or 'conchies'. Their courage has influenced anti-war activists ever since.

THE ROAD TO WAR

The reasons for war were complex. Tensions had developed in Europe fuelled by nationalism and imperialism as countries competed for more influence in the world. Germany and Britain were increasing their military strength and a complex system of military alliances and treaties had divided Europe into two opposing camps: the Triple Alliance of Germany, Austria and Italy and the Triple Entente (friendship) of France, Russia and Britain.

On 28 June 1914 a Serbian nationalist assassinated Archduke Franz Ferdinand, heir to the Austrian throne. Austria-Hungary declared war on Serbia. Russian forces mobilised to support Serbia. Germany declared war on Russia, Belgium and France. German forces marched into Belgium and, on 4 August, Britain, bound by treaty to defend Belgium, declared war on Germany. The First World War had begun.

> I **KNOW** what it is to kill a pig; I **won't** kill a **MAN.**
>
> *Stephen Winsten, conscientious objector*

A GLOBAL CONFLICT

Nearly all the world's countries were involved in the war. The conflict lasted for more than four years from 4 August 1914 until 11 November 1918. Most fighting occurred in Europe, on what became known as the Western Front, a line of trenches stretching more than 400 miles (about 700 kilometres) from the Swiss border, through France and Belgium to the North Sea. Fighting also took place in the Middle East, Africa and Asia.

A DIFFERENT KIND OF COURAGE

Many historians write about the brave soldiers who fought and died in the war. They were brave. Huddled in trenches on the Western Front or in Gallipoli (part of Turkey), constantly bombarded by shells, they risked injury and death to fight for their country. Most had little choice and by the war's end more than nine million had been killed.

Historians write less about conscientious objectors. They were brave too, although it took a different kind of courage to refuse to fight with a world at war. People thought they were cowards but conscientious objectors were not scared. They would not fight because they thought killing was wrong and they did not think any government should tell them to fight. They faced insults, brutality, imprisonment and even death. They lost their health, their friends and their jobs and spent months, and even years, in prison.

CONCHIES

The word 'conchies' is short for conscientious objectors. British newspapers first used the word in 1916 when the first conscientious objectors refused to be conscripted. It was used as an insult but some conscientious objectors (COs) described themselves as 'conchies' or 'conshies'.

AROUND THE WORLD

Conscription had existed in the US since the American Civil War (1861–65). During the First World War, American conscientious objectors could choose to serve in non-fighting units but about 2,000 men refused absolutely to serve in the army. Most were imprisoned. In New Zealand, around 2,600 men made a conscience objection to conscription, which was introduced in 1916. Many of these men were harshly treated. In Canada certain religious groups were given automatic exemption from military service.

FORCED TO FIGHT

When war was declared, patriotism and war fever swept through Britain. Men rushed to join the army but, as the war progressed, more were needed. In 1916 the government introduced conscription. Conscientious objectors prepared to refuse the call to arms.

' The first signs of **WAR MADNESS** soon appeared… the papers reported thousands of recruits **volunteering** for service. However many might volunteer yet would I not. God had not put me on the earth to go **destroying** his own children. '

John (Bert) Brocklesby

WILLING RECRUITS

In 1914 most people believed the war would end quickly – 'over by Christmas' was the popular catch-phrase. Thousands of men flocked to join the army. The British government appointed Lord Kitchener, a retired Field Marshal and military hero, as Secretary of State for War. Kitchener launched a recruiting campaign, calling for half a million men to join the army. Posters displaying his picture appeared

CONSCRIPTION IN 1914

Military conscription means that a government orders men, and sometimes women, to join the armed forces. There is no choice; it is the law. In 1914 most European countries had conscript armies. Britain, however, did not have conscription; men could choose to join the army or not.

Until the First World War most British people, even senior army personnel, thought this was right. They believed military service should be a free choice. However as the First World War progressed and more men died opinions changed and in 1916 the British government introduced military conscription for the very first time.

everywhere stating 'Your Country Needs You' – and men responded. Newspapers, the public and even churches urged men to do their duty and join up.

At first recruits poured into the army at a rate of 300,000 a month. Some joined because they thought it would be a big adventure, others because their friends were doing so. Most thought it was their patriotic duty. By January 1915 a million men had joined up, marching off to war to the sound of brass bands and cheering crowds. Only men aged 18–38 were eligible but, caught up in the enthusiasm for war, boys as young as 14 applied.

RECRUITING SLOWS DOWN

By 1915 it was clear the war would not end soon – in fact, it would last another four years. The initial enthusiasm had passed and the number of voluntary recruits was dropping, from a peak of 30,000 a day at the start of the war to 70,000 a month in 1915. The main reason for this was the rising number of dead and wounded.

Soldiers were bogged down in trenches on the Western Front and casualties were mounting. By Christmas 1914 over 177,000 British soldiers had been killed and during 1915 and 1916 casualties were far higher. By the end of 1915 the British army had lost 528,272 men, killed, wounded or missing.

And on one day alone – 1 July 1916, the first day of the Battle of the Somme – 20,000 British soldiers died and a further 40,000 were injured.

The British government knew that if it wanted to continue the war and replace the men who were dying, it had to get more men into the army. Another three million were needed. A national register was set up, whereby all adults had to register their names, age and occupation. Army recruiting officers went door-to-door, visiting eligible men and putting pressure on them to enlist voluntarily. Some did but by November 1915 it was clear that the government could no longer rely on volunteers: it would have to introduce conscription, or compulsory military service.

THE MILITARY SERVICE ACT

Conscription had not been popular in Britain, although as the war progressed the public mood was changing. Families whose sons were already in the trenches increasingly resented single men who had not chosen to go and fight. Right-wing newspapers such as the *Daily Mail* urged the government to introduce conscription so that Britain could win the war but trade unions and anti-war campaigners lobbied against it.

Parliament too was divided on the subject. There were many heated debates about conscription and some Members of Parliament (MPs), including Philip Snowden, a Quaker and pacifist, argued strongly against compulsory military service. Most MPs though, including Prime Minister Asquith, felt there was little choice so, despite some opposition, on 27 January 1916 Parliament passed the Military Service Act and conscription became law.

WHITE FEATHERS

Any man who refused to join up was seen as a shirker or coward, someone who was too scared to fight. In Britain, some women handed out white feathers – a symbol of cowardice – to men who were not in uniform. The aim was to shame them into enlisting. Feathers were even given to men home on leave or who had been wounded.

Some men were furious; others felt so humiliated that they joined up. Conscientious objectors, who refused to join the army, received many white feathers. One CO, Fenner Brockway, said he received enough white feathers to make a fan.

There are a **GREAT MANY PEOPLE** belonging to various religious denominations, or to various schools of thought, who are quite **PREPARED TO SERVE** their country in the War, but **WHO OBJECT** on conscientious grounds, **TO THE TAKING OF LIFE.**

Prime Minister Asquith, House of Commons, 5 January 1916

Under the Act, all unmarried men aged 18–41 were automatically considered to have enlisted. In the words of the Act they were 'deemed to have enlisted for general service with the colours or in the reserve', that is they all effectively became soldiers as of 2 March 1916, which is when the act came into effect. They would receive call-up papers and would be sent to a military regiment. Those who refused to accept call-up papers would certainly be fined and possibly imprisoned, though no-one was quite sure at this point. It was the very first time that conscription or compulsory military service had existed in Britain. In May conscription was widened to include married men; in 1918 during the last months of the war, the upper age limit was raised to 51.

CONSCIENCE CLAUSE

Some men were automatically exempted, or free, from conscription. They included clergymen and men who were already serving in reserve forces or the Merchant Navy. Men could also apply for exemption, particularly those who were already doing work that was considered to be vital for the national interest, such as teaching, scientific research or work for the war effort, including farming and mining.

The Act also included what was known as a 'conscience clause', whereby men could apply for exemption if they had

ANTI-WAR

Most British people supported the war but some opposed it. On 2 August 1914, two days before Britain declared war, some 10,000 people gathered in London's Trafalgar Square for a huge anti-war rally. One speaker was socialist and pacifist Keir Hardie, founder of the Independent Labour Party (ILP). He had campaigned strenuously against the war, hoping that socialists across Europe would act together to prevent it. Anti-war demonstrations also took place in France and Germany. Two days after the anti-war demonstration, Trafalgar Square was full again – this time with crowds cheering the declaration of war.

a 'conscientious objection to the undertaking of combatant service', that is if their conscience, or deeply held beliefs, would not allow them to pick up weapons and fight. The Act did not say that they would necessarily be exempted from the army but if they were considered genuine, they could be exempted from actually fighting. Tribunals were set up to test the sincerity of conscientious objectors.

> I walked up from my home to **TRAFALGAR SQUARE** – about eleven miles – took part in the demonstration, LISTENED TO KEIR HARDIE and walked home… It was quite a thrilling meeting… very definitely ANTI-WAR.
>
> *Harold Bing, aged 16, attended the big anti-war demonstration in Trafalgar Square on 2 August 1914.*

HEATED DEBATES

It may seem strange that the government included this clause in the Act when the nation was so heavily involved in war and there were some very heated debates in Parliament about it. Some MPs were completely opposed to allowing exemption for conscientious objectors; others thought it should apply only to men whose religious beliefs would not allow them to fight, such as Quakers – members of the Society of Friends, who were well known for their pacifism – a profound belief that all violence is wrong.

Prime Minister Asquith knew that conscription was controversial and was aware that some men would refuse to fight. He may also have thought that including the clause would help to overcome opposition to conscription within Parliament, and he was determined that the clause should stay in. It was therefore part of the Military Service Act when it became law.

WOMEN DIVIDED

Until shortly before the war many women had been active in fighting for the right to vote. But when war began the women's movement divided. Some activists, such as leading suffragette Emmeline Pankhurst, stopped campaigning, backed the government and threw her energies into helping to recruit men for the army and demanding the right for women to do war work.

Other women, including her daughter, Sylvia Pankhurst, and suffragist Catherine Marshall, opposed the war. Many of them switched their activities to helping conscientious objectors, all of whom were men, and their families.

OPPOSING THE ACT

Even before the Military Service Act was passed, organisations had formed to oppose conscription. Chief among these was the No-Conscription Fellowship (NCF), which was launched as early as November 1914. Founding members included socialist and journalist, Fenner Brockway, and Clifford Allen, a slim, slightly built man, who was a brilliant public speaker. Three hundred men rushed to join the new organisation; as war continued membership increased to more than 10,000. The NCF lobbied Parliament, distributed leaflets and demonstrated against conscription but despite their efforts conscription became law. Men who believed it was wrong to fight, and who were going to resist conscription, prepared themselves to take a stand as conscientious objectors.

ABSOLUTE OR ALTERNATIVE?

Some COs, known as 'absolutists', refused to compromise with conscription or militarism in any way. Their stand was absolute and most of them spent long periods of time in prison. Others, known as 'alternativists', were equally opposed to killing but would take alternative work, such as caring for the wounded or working on the land, provided it did not clash with their moral beliefs. Knowing how far to take their stand against conscription was a question that troubled many COs.

THE 'CONCHIES'

Once conscription was introduced, 16,000 men in Britain took their stand as conscientious objectors and refused to fight. There were 'conchies' in Canada, New Zealand and the United States of America, but most were in Britain. Resisting conscription took courage but COs were determined to do so, no matter what the consequences.

> Many years before the war of 1914–18, I had reached the point of view that war – ALL WAR – was **wrong, futile** and **destructive**.
>
> *Archibald Baxter*

'WE YIELD TO NO ONE in our **admiration** of the self-sacrifice, the courage and the unflagging devotion of those of **our fellow-countrymen** who have felt it their duty to take up arms. Nevertheless, we cannot undertake the same form of service… we **DENY** the right of any Government to make the **SLAUGHTER** of our fellows a bounden duty.'

No-Conscription Fellowship Manifesto, 1915

ALL WALKS OF LIFE

During the First World War only men were conscientious objectors. Women were not conscripted although they would be during the Second World War. First World War COs came from all walks of life and differing backgrounds. They included single and married men, teachers, students, scientists, clerks, librarians, engineers, artists, musicians and poets. Some came from privileged families, such as Hubert Peet, a Quaker who came from a very wealthy family but had chosen to live a simple life helping the needy. Others were from humbler origins, such as Fred Murfin, a printer from Manchester. All were of military call-up age (18–41) though most were in their twenties.

DIFFERENT REASONS

There was no such thing as a 'typical' conscientious objector: COs were all very different. What they had in common was their deeply held belief that it was wrong to kill and that no government should force them to do so. Some, such as Harold Bing, who was only 18 when he became a conscientious objector, had come from pacifist, religious or political families and had been brought up to believe killing was wrong. Others did not have that sort of upbringing and made their decision against the wishes of their families.

For each man the decision to be a conscientious objector was personal: it was based on a man's conscience, which is difficult to define, but usually means the beliefs that tell a person what is right or wrong.

Many became objectors for religious reasons. They believed that the Bible's commandment, 'thou shalt not kill', meant what it said and because of their faith would not kill. Most religious objectors were Quakers but there were also a large number of Jehovah's Witnesses, some Methodists and Anglicans. Some religious COs were disgusted by ministers in their churches, who were exempt from military service themselves yet urged young men to join the army and kill.

A large number of objectors had political reasons for refusing conscription. Most were socialists, who saw the ruling class as their enemy and all working people as their brothers. They were not prepared to take up arms against their fellow men and were determined to resist the government's attempt to make them.

Other COs just felt it was morally wrong or inhuman to kill others. Whatever their reasons – and some COs had several reasons – all COs were men of very high principles and they believed their refusal to kill was right.

FENNER BROCKWAY

The son of missionary parents, Fenner Brockway (1888–1988) was a journalist, socialist and a conscientious objector. In 1914 he helped to found the No-Conscription Fellowship (NCF) and was secretary of the national committee.

In November 1916 he was arrested for refusing conscription. He was forcibly handed over to the army, where he disobeyed orders, was court-martialled and sentenced to six-months imprisonment with hard labour.

He was re-arrested several times, spending a total of 28 months in prison. While in prison, he defied the authorities and was punished by being put into solitary confinement for eight months.

He was finally released from prison in April 1919.

Brockway served twice as a Labour MP in the House of Commons (1929–31; 1950–64).

He remained a passionate and deeply committed anti-war activist until he died.

PREPARING TO RESIST

Most people in Britain thought the war was right. Being a conscientious objector meant resisting that view. It also meant challenging the government, which had taken Britain to war. It was a very courageous thing to do. Various groups supported conscientious objectors. They included the Fellowship of Reconciliation (FoR), a Christian pacifist organisation, which was founded in 1914, the Society of Friends, and the No-Conscription Fellowship (NCF), the largest and most important group of war resisters and conscientious objectors.

> We, the members of the No-Conscription Fellowship… hereby solemnly and sincerely affirm our intention to **RESIST CONSCRIPTION**, whatever the penalties may be.
>
> *Fenner Brockway*

When the NCF began it was based in Fenner Brockway's small country cottage but by 1915 it had moved headquarters to London. A central committee was formed that included Clifford Allen as chairman, Edward Grubb, a Quaker, as treasurer, Fenner Brockway and others. Conscientious objectors also set up local NCF branches all over Britain. Teacher, David Thomas, for instance formed an NCF branch in North Wales.

In 1915 the NCF issued a manifesto stating that its members would resist conscription if it were introduced. Once conscription became law NCF chiefs swung into action, leading thousands of conscientious objectors in what became known as the CO movement. Plans were drawn up and the leadership organised conventions where members discussed the best ways of resisting conscription, and also what would happen to them when they did so. In 1916 the NCF started publishing a weekly newspaper, *Tribunal*, which included NCF policy, letters and detailed information about what was happening to COs around the country.

ATTACKS AND SURVEILLANCE

The British public thought conscientious objectors were cowards or even traitors. People simply could not understand how men could refuse to fight when their country was at war.

WAVING HANKIES

In April 1916 the No-Conscription Fellowship held a two-day convention in London. About 2,000 conscientious objectors attended to listen to speakers and discuss ways of resisting conscription. An angry crowd gathered outside, shouting insults and threatening to break into the building. Every time objectors inside the building clapped, the mob outside, which could hear them, got angrier. NCF chairman Clifford Allen suggested objectors should wave their handkerchiefs rather than clapping. Every time a speaker stood up, he was greeted by thousands of fluttering white hankies – it was an extraordinary sight.

Objectors were attacked in the street and angry mobs broke up their meetings. The families of conscientious objectors also experienced a great deal of hostility. Newspapers whipped up hatred describing conscientious objectors as the 'save-their-own-skin brigade', 'won't-fight funks' or 'Hun-lovers', 'Hun' being the British nickname for Germans.

Horatio Bottomley, a right-wing journalist, called for Fenner Brockway to be imprisoned in the Tower of London. MPs in the House of Commons criticised COs and described the NCF as a 'seditious' or traitorous organisation. As the war progressed the police frequently raided the NCF offices but office staff cleverly learned to hide pamphlets and files or get them out of the office in secret. Some newspapers, such as the *Manchester Guardian*, and pacifist MPs in the House of Commons, such as Philip Snowden, spoke out in support of conscientious objectors but as the death toll continued to rise on the Western Front, few people had much sympathy for 'conchies'.

> The building was attacked… and in order not to provoke, instead of applause by clapping our hands or cheering with our voices, everyone at that conference just shook their handkerchiefs.
>
> *Fenner Brockway*

SINCERE MEN

Under the Military Service Act, men were allowed to apply for exemption from combat on grounds of conscientious objection and around 16,000 did so. No matter what the press and public threw at them, conscientious objectors knew they were sincere in their beliefs. However, knowing they were sincere was not enough: their sincerity had to be tested by tribunals, which would decide if they were genuine or not.

CLEVER STRATEGY

At first conscientious objectors were not certain what would happen to them but the leaders of the NCF laid careful plans.

Suspecting that most of them would be arrested – which is what happened – each member of the central committee had a 'shadow', someone who would step in and carry on their work while they were in prison.

Many of these substitutes were women who had been active in the suffragette movement and were highly skilled at evading the police.

'**LOOK!**
CHRIST IN KHAKI,
out in France thrusting His
bayonet into the body of a German
workman. See! The Son of God
with a machine gun, ambushing a
column of German infantry…
NO! NO! That picture is an
impossible one…
**I CANNOT UPHOLD
THE WAR**…'

Dr Alfred Salter

ARCHIBALD BAXTER

A New Zealand pacifist, Archibald Baxter (1881-1970) was a conscientious objector during the First World War. In 1916 when New Zealand introduced conscription, he refused to serve in the army. He was arrested and taken with other COs by ship from New Zealand to France. The men refused to wear their uniforms and were stripped naked and left on deck. Once in France Baxter, his brother and the other New Zealanders were beaten, starved and brutalised in an attempt to force them to become soldiers. Baxter was placed on his own in an area that was being shelled. Baxter suffered dreadful physical and mental damage but would not submit. In 1939 he published an account of his experiences called *We Will Not Cease*.

TRIBUNALS

When conscription came COs applied for exemption from military service. They had to appear before tribunals, most of which treated them very badly.

APPLYING FOR EXEMPTION

From February 1916 the War Office began sending out call-up papers for eligible men to join the army. Now conscientious objectors had to make a big decision: would they ignore the call up and wait to be arrested as deserters? Or would they make a formal application for exemption on grounds of conscience?

' A man who would not help to defend his country and womankind is a coward and a cad. '

Salford Tribunal

About 1,200 conscientious objectors flatly refused to apply for exemption because they did not agree with any part of the process. However, the majority of objectors did apply. They filled in an official form on which they gave their reasons for refusing to fight. Their statements varied: some were short; others were long and detailed. Explanations included religious or political beliefs. Objectors sent off their forms and in due course received a letter telling them to appear before a local tribunal.

More than 2,000 tribunals were set up around Britain. Their job was to test the sincerity of conscientious objectors. They also had the legal right to decide what should happen to the objector after the tribunal. There were appeal tribunals which an objector could apply to if he was unhappy with the decision of his local tribunal.

TRIBUNALS

Most tribunals consisted of a group of five or six men. Local councils chose the tribunal members, who included tradesmen, clergymen, council officials, bank managers and a trade union representative. Occasionally a woman sat on the panel. Tribunal members had no legal training and, because they were too old to join the army, were much older than the conscientious objectors who appeared before them.

A military representative, appointed by the War Office, was also present. This was a retired army officer or recruiting officer, who was not part of the tribunal and could not vote but he could give advice and was very influential. Usually dressed in khaki, military representatives saw it as their duty to get men into the army: they intimidated applicants and could appeal if they did not like a tribunal's decision.

Tribunal hearings were held in town halls, magistrate courts and other official buildings. They were open to the press and the public, usually a conscientious objector's friends and family, but some hearings were held in private.

'The tribunals seem to take the view that a **conscientious objector**, whatever his statement of belief, is a person to be REBUKED, BULLIED and CONDEMNED.'

Tribunal

QUESTIONS AND ANSWERS

Very few official records of conscientious objectors' tribunals exist today. Fortunately for us John (Bert) Brocklesby, who appeared at his local tribunal in Doncaster on 29 February 1916, wrote an account. Here is part of it.

Chairman: If the Germans were attacking Doncaster, if you could save the lives of some women and children, would you do so?

Brocklesby: I would try to save life, but not by taking life.

Chairman: Would you not shoot any Germans?

Brocklesby: No sir.

Chairman: Would you knock any down?

Brocklesby: Perhaps.

Chairman: If you would not take life to save the lives of hundreds of women and children, you would be responsible for their deaths.

Tribunal member: Would you be prepared to take non-combatant service, say in a munitions factory or mine-sweeping?

Brocklesby: No sir, they would not let me sweep English mines as well as German mines.

Clerk: It seems as if he [Brocklesby] has an objection to doing anything that would take him into danger.

Brocklesby: It is very difficult to bring evidence to prove a conscientious objection: one can only prove it by suffering from it. I am prepared to die for my principles. I am fighting for the principle of freedom of conscience for every Englishman... It would be a pity if, while there are so many thousands who are ready to die for their country, there are not some who are prepared to die for higher principles.

Chairman: Are you a local preacher?

Brocklesby: Yes.

Chairman: Well, you had better go and preach somewhere else.

APPEARING AT A TRIBUNAL

For most objectors, appearing before a tribunal was like being on trial although none of the tribunal members were judges or lawyers. Tribunal members sat at a table and the objector appeared before them. The tribunal chairman and other members asked questions, often about the objector's written statement, then decided whether they thought the CO was genuine.

' My case was heard on March 23rd. **IT WAS A TERRIBLE ORDEAL** for anyone sensitive; I found it very trying. **HOW DOES ONE** feel when trying, in public, to **CONVINCE PEOPLE**, who are out to misconstrue everything one says, that because of one's religious convictions – no matter what the consequences – **NO WAR SERVICE IS POSSIBLE?** '

Fred Murfin

VEGETARIAN

'At Salford a conscientious objector said he was a vegetarian. The military representative said they were not asking for cannibals to eat the enemy; they wanted fighters!'

Tribunal, Wednesday, 15 March, 1916

Some hearings lasted an hour or so, others were over within a few minutes. Sometimes objectors did not even get the chance to say anything and were unable to explain their reasons for objecting to war and killing.

LITTLE CHANCE OF A FAIR HEARING

The government had stated that tribunals should give conscientious objectors a fair hearing. Members of the tribunal were not supposed to let their personal feelings about COs influence their decisions. But tribunals supported the war. Like the British public, they thought conscientious objectors were unpatriotic cowards who were just trying to get out of the army. They simply could not understand why able-bodied men would refuse to fight for their country and were completely baffled by conscientious objectors' deeply held belief that killing was wrong. As a result conscientious objectors had very little chance of a fair hearing.

HOSTILE TREATMENT

Most conscientious objectors had a hard time at their tribunals; the experience was unpleasant and humiliating. Some objectors were confident and able to express themselves easily. Others were very nervous and found the experience upsetting. Nearly all COs found it very difficult to explain their anti-war beliefs to people who did not really want to listen to them. After all, as many objectors commented: how does a man prove he has a conscience?

One objector after another found himself facing hostility from tribunals and military representatives. Tribunal members deliberately misunderstood what objectors told them. They bullied, insulted and ridiculed objectors, showing them no respect and accusing them of being cowards. One tribunal chairman, Councillor Hopwood of the Shaw tribunal, accused a CO of being 'nothing but a shivering mass of unwholesome fat'. The man Councillor Hopwood insulted was in fact a highly respected research scientist. Another CO was told he was not sincere in his belief that killing was wrong because he had admitted to eating cheese, which involved 'killing the maggots' – a very odd statement but typical of how tribunals treated objectors. Some questions had nothing to do with a man's beliefs but were designed to humiliate. One objector was asked if he washed regularly, and when he replied that he did was told that it did not appear so.

Tribunal members also threw trick questions at conscientious objectors to confuse them. One common question was to ask a man what he would do if he saw someone attacking his mother or sister. Answering this question was very difficult: if the objector said he would hit the attacker, then the tribunal panel said he was not a genuine conscientious objector. If he said he would do nothing, he was told he had no decent feelings. Many conscientious

> I AM A CHRISTIAN and a Socialist. Believing in the Gospels… I am profoundly convinced that the work of war is opposed to their teaching… I CANNOT AND WILL NOT KILL.
>
> *Walter Ayles*

"I am **CONSCIENTIOUSLY OPPOSED** to everything that destroys human life. I know nothing in the world that is so precious as human life, **and** I **CANNOT FEEL JUSTIFIED**, under any circumstances, **IN DESTROYING MEN'S LIVES**."

David Thomas

objectors were told they were too young to have a conscience and several were accused of being unpatriotic although the truth was that COs loved their country but believed in peace rather than war.

Religious objectors had a slightly easier time. Tribunal members could understand a man saying that the Bible said it was wrong to kill. But even then, many tribunals challenged religious objectors with quotes from the Bible that said the reverse. Tribunals had no sympathy at all for political objectors; they did not think that anyone who gave political reasons for refusing to kill was a genuine conscientious objector and gave them a very hard time.

OUTCOMES

After questioning an objector, the tribunal made its decision. Tribunals could make one of four decisions: they could give an objector absolute exemption from military service. They could let a man off from military service, provided he did civilian work of national importance, such as farming or hospital work. They could release a man from combatant (fighting) service only and send him into a non-combatant (non-fighting) unit in the army. Or they could reject the application completely and order the objector to join a fighting unit immediately.

No matter what the law said, tribunals did not want to let objectors off military service. Some tribunals did not even think the government should have made allowance for conscientious objection. As a result only a few men were granted complete exemption, most of them Quakers. Tribunals sent most objectors into non-fighting units in the army, or into work of national importance. They rejected about 2,000 applicants, sending those objectors straight into combatant units.

For conscientious objectors resistance did not end with the tribunal; now they had to decide whether to accept a tribunal's decision or disobey it.

'The Military Representative asked if I would kill wild beasts. I replied, "The GERMANS ARE NOT WILD BEASTS, sir!"…'

Fred Murfin

RELIGIOUS EXEMPTION

In Canada, under the 1917 Military Service Act, conscientious objectors could claim exemption from combat if they were members of what were known as the 'peace churches', such as Quakers and Mennonites. They had to appear before a tribunal to prove their sincerity. Many tribunals saw these men as cowards and shirkers but most received exemption. Non-religious COs were usually imprisoned for up to two years. In January 1919 more than 100 Canadian COs were still in prison.

BEATEN AND ABUSED IN THE USA

Military conscription was first introduced into the USA during the American Civil War (1861–65). It was introduced again in 1917 when America entered the First World War. Many COs were posted to non-fighting units but around 2,000 or more absolutists refused to have anything to do with the military. They were sent to military prisons such as Fort Leavenworth, Kansas. Like their British counterparts, they were dreadfully brutalised. They were beaten, kicked, hung by their wrists, forced to exercise, drenched in freezing showers and beaten with belts and scrubbing brushes until they bled. Abuse was so severe that two men died and one committed suicide. Alternativists worked on the land and some served in France with the American Friends Service Committee, helping the wounded.

▶ *This famous image shows the Secretary of State for War, Lord Kitchener. It first appeared on 5 September 1914 on the cover of* London Opinion *magazine and later inspired army recruitment posters.Once war had been declared, young men were under massive pressure to volunteer for military service. See page 12.*

▲ *Scottish socialist and labour leader Keir Hardie speaks at an anti-war demonstration in Trafalgar Square, London, on 2 August 1914, just two days before Britain declared war. Hardie was an outspoken pacifist. See page 19.*

THE CONSCIENTIOUS OBJECTOR AT THE FRONT!

WHILE THE SHOT AND SHELL ARE FLYING
AND THE MIGHTY CANNONS BOOM
HE IS TIDYING UP THE TRENCHES WITH
A DUST-PAN AND A BROOM!

▲ Popular cartoons such as this one mocked COs, portraying them as weak, effeminate and lacking in courage. However, far from having an easy time, COs faced both the contempt of the public and brutal official punishments. They needed to be very tough to stand up for their principles.

► In this recruiting poster, the designer Savile Lumley forces the viewer to imagine the shame of having to answer this question in post-war Britain. The poster was so emotionally manipulative that Lumley did not wish to be associated with it at the time.

Daddy, what did YOU do in the Great War?

◀ *Prominent CO Fenner Brockway helped found the No-Conscription Fellowship in 1914. Forced into the army, he endured court-martial and imprisonment for his principles. This statue of Brockway stands in Red Lion Square, London. See page 27.*

▶ *The printed manifesto of the No-Conscription Fellowship sets out the principles for which COs were prepared to endure imprisonment and even risk their lives.*

MANIFESTO

ISSUED BY THE

NO-CONSCRIPTION FELLOWSHIP

The case for and against compulsory military and munition service is being argued by many who, for reasons of age or sex, would not be subject to it. The signatories to this Manifesto think it imperative to voice a protest in the name of a large body of men in this country who, though able-bodied and of military age, will—in the event of coercive measures—be bound by deep conscientious conviction to decline these services, whatever the consequences of refusal.

We yield to no one in our admiration of the self-sacrifice, the courage and the unflagging devotion of those of our fellow-countrymen who have felt it their duty to take up arms. Nevertheless, we cannot undertake the same form of service; our conviction is solemn and unalterable.

Whatever the purpose to be achieved by war, however high the ideals for which belligerent nations may struggle, for us "Thou shalt not kill" means what it says. The destruction of our fellow-men—young men like ourselves—appals us; we cannot assist in the cutting-off of one generation from life's opportunities. Insistence upon individual obligations in the interests of national well-being has no terrors for us; we gladly admit—we would even extend—the right of the community to impose duties upon its members for the common good, but we deny the right of any Government to make the slaughter of our fellows a bounden duty.

We have been brought to this standpoint by many ways. Some of us have reached it through the Christian faith in which we have been reared, and to our interpretation of which we plead the right to stand loyal. Others have found it by association with international movements; we believe in the solidarity of the human race, and we cannot betray the ties of brotherhood which bind us to one another throughout the nations of the world.

All of us, however we may have come to this conviction, believe in the value and sacredness of human personality, and are prepared to sacrifice as much in the cause of the world's peace as our fellows are sacrificing in the cause of the nation's war.

Believing it is the imperative duty of every citizen to serve his country, we are eager to render national service through such occupations as shall help to build up the life and strength of our country, without inflicting suffering upon other people.

We have not emphasised the objections to Conscription which are widely held by many who do not share our views on war. There are many who are now exposing the folly of forced service from the military standpoint; there is the vast body of Trade Unionists who view with suspicion the agitation of the National Service League and the Conscriptionist Press, and see in it a menace to the working class; there are experts who demonstrate that the revolution entailed would undermine the financial and commercial stability which is not the least valuable asset this country offers to the Allied Powers; there are the advocates of national unity who for that reason alone deprecate the raising of so disruptive an issue; and finally there are those whose objections are held on the ground of the great traditions and liberties of our country.

We, too, recognise to the full the grave dangers to those liberties and those traditions in the present agitation for Conscription, and especially as it must affect the workers of the nation, but first and foremost our decision rests on the ground of the serious violation of moral and religious convictions which a system of compulsion must involve.

We believe the real inspiration that prompts all efforts towards progress is a desire that human life may become of more account. This ideal we cannot renounce; its claim is absolute.

(Signed)

CLIFFORD ALLEN, Chairman.
EDWARD GRUBB, Hon. Treasurer.
A. FENNER BROCKWAY, Hon. Secretary.

A. BARRATT BROWN
A. SUTHERLAND CAMPBELL
W. J. CHAMBERLAIN
J. H. HUDSON   } Committee.
MORGAN JONES
C. H. NORMAN
LEYTON RICHARDS (REV.)

Merton House,
Salisbury Square.

► *This 1916 newspaper clipping shows prominent COs giving themselves up to police.*

Councillor Ayles (A), J. P. Fletcher (B), W. J. Chamberlain (C), Clifford Allen (D), and A. Fenner Brockway (E), five no-conscriptionists, all of whom, except Allen, gave themselves up to the police yesterday.

"And what work are you doing of National Importance?"
"Why, I'm rearin' eight children an' helping to make airyplanes!"

▲ *Another cartoon portraying COs as pathetic shirkers who wished to get out of 'doing their duty', this time by seaside postcard artist Donald McGill. Tribunals consisted of important members of the local community as well as a military representative. As such they were usually hostile to COs. See page 36.*

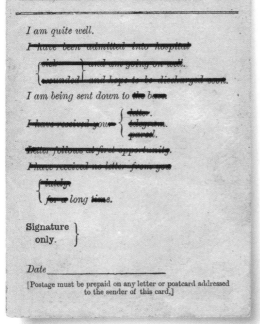

NOTHING is to be written on this except the date and signature of the sender. Sentences not required may be erased. If anything else is added the post card will be destroyed.

I am quite well.

~~I have been admitted into hospital~~

~~{ sick } and am going on well.~~
~~{ wounded } and hope to be discharged soon.~~

I am being sent down to ~~the base~~.

~~I have received your~~ ~~{ letter.~~
~~{ telegram.~~
~~{ parcel.~~

~~Letter follows at first opportunity.~~

~~I have received no letter from you~~

~~{ lately.~~
{ for a long ~~time~~.

Signature only. }

Date _____

[Postage must be prepaid on any letter or postcard addressed to the sender of this card.]

◀ CO John Brocklesby managed to send this military postcard to his family to let them know where he was. These cards were intended as a way for soldiers to let their families know they were alive after a battle. Brocklesby cleverly adapted the text to read ' I am quite well. I am being sent down to b long (Boulogne, France). See page 55.

▶ An illustration from a military manual showing how soldiers could be brutally tied to a fence or other object as a punishment for repeatedly disobeying orders. This punishment was imposed on many COs. See page 56.

▲ *This photograph shows 15 of the Harwich 'Frenchmen', who were sentenced to death, commuted to ten years' hard labour, by military court-martial. See page 59.*

◀ *One of the tiny, hand-made newspapers produced by imprisoned COs using smuggled materials. See page 68.*

▲ *A large group of COs photographed at Dyce Work Camp, near Aberdeen, in October 1916. Living conditions there became so appalling that the camp was eventually shut down. See page 77.*

▲ *COs working at Princetown Work Centre (Dartmoor prison) as part of the Home Office Scheme. As at Dyce, living conditions were very poor and the COs there had a very hard time. See pages 78-9.*

◀ *This memorial plaque commemorating the sacrifice and courage of COs is at the headquarters of the Peace Pledge Union in London. See page 90.*

▼ *In 1994 this memorial to all COs worldwide was unveiled in London's Tavistock Square.*

INTO THE ARMY

Tribunals sent more than 7,500 conscientious objectors into the army. However, the objectors resisted all attempts to turn them into soldiers. They were brutally punished and threatened with death – but they refused to submit.

IGNORING THE CALL UP

Once their tribunals were over, conscientious objectors who had been directed into the army had to decide whether they would accept the situation or not. Most decided to resist.

Some ignored call-up notices telling them to report to their regiments. They stayed at home and were arrested and taken under escort into the army.

DEEMED TO BE SOLDIERS

Under the Military Service Act, 1916, any man of military age, who had not been granted exemption from military service, was considered to be a soldier, whether he wanted to be or not. Conscientious objectors who were sent into the army insisted they were civilians; the army said they were soldiers.

> **We will refuse to obey all military orders on conscientious grounds.**
>
> *Fred Murfin*

Others accepted their call-up notices, made their way to their army units and then began to disobey orders. Either way, conscientious objectors refused to regard themselves as soldiers.

NON-COMBATANT CORPS

About 2,500 conscientious objectors were sent into military combatant or fighting units. Another 5,000 were directed into non-combatant duties within the army.

In March 1916 a special Non-Combatant Corps (NCC) was created for conscientious objectors. The press nicknamed it the 'No-Courage Corps'. Officers were from the regular army but otherwise most of the men were conscientious objectors, who were given the rank of private. They had to wear khaki army uniform and were trained in drilling and other army procedures but did not have to carry weapons or fight. Their duties included repairing roads, digging latrines and building huts and baths for fighting soldiers.

The government thought the NCC would be an ideal solution. Conscientious objectors would not have to fight but they could do useful work for the army. However, both the government and the army failed to understand that it did not matter whether an army unit was combatant or non-combatant: on moral grounds conscientious objectors would not accept conscription and military service.

RESISTING ORDERS

Once in the army conscientious objectors began to resist. Some refused the medical examination that all soldiers had to undergo, or would not put on uniforms. They disobeyed other commands such as marching or saluting. They were perfectly polite but refused to do what they were told. Fenner Brockway, for instance, remained sitting when the commanding officer walked into the room; soldiers around him leapt to their feet and stood at attention.

For the army this type of resistance was new: conscription had not existed before so they had never encountered conscientious objectors. Many army officers had no idea how to deal with this new group of men who believed in peace and would not fight.

Some officers tried persuasion, encouraging COs to accept army discipline and offering comfortable duties in the army. Objectors politely refused. Others used force to try to intimidate objectors into accepting army discipline.

BRUTAL PUNISHMENTS

Disobeying orders was a serious offence, leading to punishment and ultimately court-martial. Most officers handed out brutal punishments to COs who refused orders. Objectors were manhandled, forcibly dressed in uniforms, and beaten. One conscientious objector, George Dutch, who was a Quaker and a socialist, was posted to Maxton Camp near Dover. He refused to put on his uniform. The major ordered him to be stripped, placed in a tent and left with his uniform next to him.

> I was **FROZEN RIGHT THROUGH** with exposure… I just sat there and set my teeth to **STICK WHATEVER CAME.**
>
> *George Dutch*

After a day or two the tent was moved to the top of a cliff overlooking the sea. The sides of the tent were rolled up and Dutch was left inside, dressed only in vest and pants, with his uniform next to him. It was November and bitterly cold. Regular soldiers in the unit were sympathetic but none were allowed to approach him. Dutch remained in the tent for ten days and nights in the bitter cold but still refused to put on his uniform. Eventually medical personnel intervened and he was taken back to camp.

As resistance continued, so punishments became more severe. At Harwich Redoubt, an old fortress, conscientious objectors who refused orders were strapped into straitjackets and made to stand in the hot sun for hours. Some were locked into punishment cells. Moisture trickled down the walls, there was little light and men were kept without food for three days.

Conscientious objectors were frequently dragged around parade grounds, kicked and punched. One man, James Brightmore, was posted to an army unit in Cleethorpes. Refusing orders, he was sentenced to 28 days solitary confinement and placed in a damp pit, 10 ft deep and 3 ft wide (3 m x 0.9 m). The pit was so wet he had to stand on duckboards and there was no room to sit down. A friendly soldier smuggled him some food.

SENTENCED TO DEATH

In May and June 1916 punishment and intimidation reached new heights when a number of conscientious objectors were taken in secret from England to France where they were sentenced to death.

Fifty men in three separate groups were taken out of punishment cells from Harwich Redoubt, Richmond Castle in Yorkshire, and Seaford Camp, Sussex. They were handcuffed, taken by train to Southampton and from there by ship to Le Havre, France. All of them knew that once in the war zone, there was a strong possibility they might be shot for refusing orders. Even so, once in France, the men began disobeying orders. Seventeen of them were sent onto a vast parade ground among 1,000 soldiers, and orders were given to drill. Not a single conscientious objector moved: according to those who took part it was an extraordinary and thrilling sight to see conscientious objectors making their stand.

A LUCKY NOTE

As objectors were being taken by train to Southampton, someone managed to throw a note out of the window telling whoever read it that COs were being taken to France. The information reached the No-Conscription Fellowship and sympathetic individuals went straight to Prime Minister Henry Asquith. Knowing nothing about the events, Asquith was shocked and sent a telegram to the army's commander in chief saying the objectors should not be shot without government approval. Later John Brocklesby, using a coded postcard, managed to let his family know that he and others were in France.

Objectors were beaten, bullied and manhandled as the army used every method it knew to try to break their resistance. Some of the Harwich objectors were moved to a field punishment unit at Harfleur and given 28 days field punishment. The most brutal punishment in the army, this involved strapping a man to a rigid object, such as a post or gun carriage wheel, and stretching out his arms in the shape of a crucifix. Tied tightly the man could not move and was left like this for two hours, once a day for three days. Following a break, the punishment was repeated for another three days and so on until the 28 days were completed.

'We were placed with our FACES TO THE BARBED WIRE of the inner fence. As the ROPES with which we were tied fastened AROUND THE BARBED WIRE instead of the usual thick wooden post… when I wished to turn my head I had to do so very cautiously to avoid my face being torn by the barbs…'

Harry Stanton, sentenced to field punishment

In June 1916 the objectors were moved to Boulogne, France, where they faced a court-martial. On 15 June the first four men were taken out onto the parade ground to hear their sentences. The officer in charge read out the men's 'crimes', which included disobedience and failure to obey commands and then announced the sentence: death by firing squad. Not one of the objectors flinched. Pausing for a few seconds, the officer then announced that the death sentence was commuted to ten years' imprisonment with hard labour. The army's attempt to break the conscientious objectors' determined resistance had failed.

Over the next two days 35 out of the 50 COs were marched onto the parade ground, sentenced to death and then told the sentence had been changed to ten years' hard labour. Soon afterwards 'the Frenchmen', as they were later known, were sent first to the military prison in Rouen, where they continued disobeying orders, and then back to England to begin their prison sentences.

'We have been warned today that we are **NOW WITHIN THE WAR ZONE**… the military authorities have absolute power and disobedience may be followed by very **SEVERE PENALTIES**… possibly the death penalty… **DO NOT BE DOWNHEARTED** if the worst comes to the worst; many have died cheerfully before for a worse cause.'

Stuart Beavis

THE 'FRENCHMEN'

The 35 men sentenced to death were:

Cornelius Barritt

Stuart Beavis

Bernard Bonner

H F Brewster

John (Bert) Brocklesby

Clifford Cartwright

E C Cryer

Alfred Evans

Jack Foster

W T Frear

Norman Gaudie

Clarence Hall

Stafford Hall

Geoffrey Hicks

Rowland Jackson

P B Jordan

Herbert Law

William Law

R A Lown

Howard Marten

Alfred Martlew

Fred Murfin

Alfred Myers

Adam Priestly

Leonard Renton

Oscar Ricketts

John Ring

John Routledge

Harry Scullard

Herbert Senior

Ernest Spencer

Harold Stanton

Alfred Tayler

Edwin Walker

A F Walling

'As I stood listening to the sentences… the feeling of **JOY AND TRIUMPH** surged up within me… **I FELT PROUD** to have the privilege of being one of that small company of COs **TESTIFYING TO A TRUTH** which the world as yet had not grasped…

one of the 'Frenchmen'

PRISON

More than 6,000 conscientious objectors were sent to prison. Some spent months in prison, others as long as three years. Objectors suffered physical and mental hardship but continued to stick to their principles.

ARRESTS

The first arrests took place within days of conscription being introduced. In April 1916 the No-Conscription Fellowship (NCF) reported in *Tribunal* that 30 of their members had been arrested; by May 1916 the number had risen to 700. By the early part of 1917 more than 3,000 had been arrested. Eventually numbers reached 6,100.

> '**Funny. You're in for murder and I'm in here for refusing to.**'
>
> *Caption to cartoon of conscientious objector speaking to a 'lifer'.*

Most objectors were sent to prison following a court-martial, or military court. Sentences usually varied from 112 days with hard labour to two years, the harshest sentence possible then (short of the death sentence). One conscientious objector, Hubert Peet, later wrote a pamphlet about his experiences called *112 Days' Hard Labour*.

Although COs were sentenced by a military court, most served their time in civilian prisons. These included Wormwood Scrubs, Wandsworth, Pentonville, Winchester, Maidstone and Walton Prison, in Liverpool. This meant that conscientious objectors, men who were refusing to kill, served their time alongside men who had been convicted of murder and other violent crimes.

PRISON LIFE

Conditions in prison were harsh, not just for conscientious objectors but for all prisoners, though for objectors who had never been anywhere near a prison, conditions came as something of a shock. On arrival objectors were questioned, given a medical examination, put through a tepid bath, and then given their prison clothes. These consisted of flannel vest and pants, cotton shirt and the regulation uniform of khaki stamped with large black arrows. Prisoners were also given a number, usually the number of their cell.

Each objector was put into a single cell, which was small and basic. It contained only a plank bed, a small table, a chamber pot and a can for water. Food was eaten in the cell, and cutlery consisted of a plate, a knife (made of bendable tin), fork and spoon. There was a window high up in the wall. Warders could spy on objectors through a small peep-hole in the door. Tacked to the door was a list of rules; prisoners who broke any of them were punished.

Cells were poorly heated and ventilated. In winter they were damp and freezing. Many objectors developed bronchitis, flu and tuberculosis. In summer when warders unlocked the cell door they found objectors who had fainted from the heat.

EXPLAINING TO CHILDREN

Hubert Peet, Quaker and journalist, spent a total of three years in prison. His wife and three small children missed him dreadfully. Writing materials were limited but he wrote to his children explaining why he was away and describing his cell:

'... it is difficult for you to understand why I am not at home with you... I would if I could but I am not allowed to... The English people and the German people have got angry with each other like two children who want the same toys and hundreds of men are trying to kill each other... Mummy and Daddy... think it is wrong even if another person gets angry with you, for you to get angry with them... This is why your daddy says he cannot be a soldier and go and try and kill the daddies of little German boys and girls. Most people think he ought to go and because he will not... they are shutting him up in prison...'

FIRST MONTH

For the first month objectors were allowed no contact with anyone apart from the warder. They were not allowed any letters, visitors, or any books other than the Bible, a prayer book and an educational book. They were locked into their cells for 23 hours a day, being allowed out only for a brief exercise period and to slop out their chamber pot.

After a month, they could work with other prisoners; after two months they could send and receive one letter a month and were allowed a monthly visit. They could also take books from the prison library.

'EVERY MAN you have shut away in prison for remaining true to his sense of right and wrong HAS GATHERED A COURAGE and quiet determination.'
Clifford Allen

FOOD AND WORK

The prison day was monotonous. It began around 6 am with slopping out and tidying the cell. Work consisted of sewing mailbags, something that conscientious objectors had no experience of at all. Eventually an objector might move on to working on the prison laundry or a workshop, perhaps making shoes. Food was dreadful consisting mainly of poorly cooked meat, bacon fat, potatoes, beans and watery porridge. Several COs commented that they often found mouse droppings in their meals and, when they had any salad, it was full of slugs and dirt. Many COs were vegetarian but it was a while before prison authorities made allowance for their diets by including some cheese.

BREAKING THE RULES

It was absolutely forbidden for prisoners to talk to each other. For objectors who were used to chatting and debating, the silence rule was one of the worst things about prison. Anyone caught talking was punished, usually with a period of solitary confinement on a punishment diet of bread and water.

Conscientious objectors though were clever people and they found ways of communicating. Using a type of Morse code, they tapped out the alphabet on pipes running through their cell walls so that they were able to communicate with friends in other cells. One objector acted as a kind of switchboard operator, receiving messages and passing them on to men in other cells. Some objectors became so good at this prison code that they even used it for playing chess with friends, tapping out moves on the pipes.

To see all around you human beings like yourself and **NOT TO BE ABLE TO SPEAK** to them is the most inhuman punishment... It is **CRUEL** and **HEARTLESS**.

Mark Hayler

SUPPORT FROM OUTSIDE

Outside the prison walls, friends and family did what they could to support conscientious objectors and the families left behind. The No-Conscription Fellowship (NCF) sent observers to tribunals and organised prison visitors. Dorothy Bing, sister of conscientious objector Harold Bing, went with others to sing Christmas carols outside the walls of

TINY NEWSPAPERS

Right under the prison warders' noses, conscientious objectors in every prison produced tiny newspapers, using rough sheets of toilet paper and smuggled-in ink and pencil leads. The newspapers, which rarely measured more than 12 cm (5 in) square, included articles, poems, drawings, items of news and many jokes. It was a remarkable achievement.

Wormwood Scrubs. Harold and his comrades waved their window blinds to show they had heard. Local NCF branches also organised socials and outings for the wives and children of conscientious objectors.

RESISTING THE AUTHORITIES

As months passed some conscientious objectors – the absolutists – began to defy prison rules, including the silence rule. While at Walton Prison, Fenner Brockway and others decided they would speak openly and for ten days objectors talked to each other, held debates and organised concerts. Punishment was severe. Brockway was given eight months in solitary confinement, the first three months on bread and water alone. Members of Sinn Fein (Irish republicans) in the same prison arranged for newspapers to be smuggled in for him. Brockway believed this saved him from going mad.

Other objectors, including Clifford Allen, chairman of the NCF, went on hunger and work strikes, refusing to do prison work or eat as a protest against their confinement or mistreatment. Again the punishments were severe. Many were forcibly fed, a horrific process that involved a tube being forced through an objector's nose into his throat while liquid food was poured through. One objector, W E Burns, choked to death because the liquid went into his lungs.

'CAT AND MOUSE'

Some absolutists served many imprisonments under what was known as the 'cat and mouse' procedure. The end of a prison sentence did not mean freedom. Instead, when an objector was released, he was still 'deemed' to be a soldier so was sent back into the army just as before. The absolutist began disobeying orders again, was punished, court-martialled and sent back to prison. Under the 'cat and mouse' treatment some objectors served as many as five prison sentences.

COMRADESHIP AND ISOLATION

As war continued, soldiers in the trenches began to believe the war would never end. Similarly conscientious objectors going back into prison again and again began to believe prison would never end. Most of them suffered illness, dizziness, weight loss and found it increasingly difficult to concentrate. Most conscientious objectors were sociable people; they were used to meetings and debates. Being shut away from the outside world took its toll. But they were men of principle. However hard it got, they would not give in. A deep comradeship developed between the men that helped them to survive.

'To some **PRISON WAS HELL**... days never end and nights never end... you can bang your head against the wall... Men would shout out in the night, anything to break the monotony... it seemed as if there would **NEVER BE AN END** to it.

Mark Hayler

ALTERNATIVE SERVICE

Conscientious objectors believed it was morally wrong to kill but not all were absolutists. Some were prepared to accept official war work, provided it was not linked to killing. Thousands worked on the land, producing food, or worked in hospitals in Britain and France.

A DIFFICULT CHOICE

Conscientious objectors faced difficult choices: should they appear before a tribunal or not? Should they disobey orders or not? How far should they take their principled stand?

The leadership of the No-Conscription Fellowship (NCF), including Clifford Allen and Fenner Brockway, believed in taking an absolute stand and were not prepared to accept anything the government told them to do.

Other objectors were not able to be absolutists. Some had wives and families and were worried they would suffer financially if they went to prison. Several did not have the confidence to take an absolutist stand. Either way, some objectors accepted non-combatant duties in the army and others accepted civilian work.

WORK OF NATIONAL IMPORTANCE

Tribunals let off 6,500 conscientious objectors from military service, provided they did work of 'national importance'. The COs had to find the work, which had to be approved by the tribunals. Naturally COs would not work in munitions factories, making shells and weapons of war, or do other work that helped the war, so the government drew up a list of approved occupations. These included work on the land, fruit growing, labouring, working with transport, including the railways, and hospital work.

Many COs had been in skilled or professional jobs before the war but tribunals rarely allowed them to stay in them. Instead most conscientious objectors were placed in hard physical and menial work, which often meant that a teacher ploughed up fields or an accountant worked in a bakery.

There was one major difficulty. Employers, such as farmers, did not always want to give conscientious objectors a job because they despised them. Local councils too would not employ conscientious objectors, and sacked many, particularly those who had worked as teachers. They believed that COs would spread pacifist ideas to young children.

Eventually the government persuaded farmers and others to use conscientious objectors as workers. By the end of the war, hundreds if not thousands of COs were working on the land, ploughing, digging, hedging, planting and harvesting. It was hard work and not what the men were used to but many enjoyed country life and felt they were helping to produce the nation's food. Others worked in mines, in welfare work, helping the poor and needy, and as orderlies in hospitals.

EQUALITY OF SACRIFICE

The government believed that just as soldiers had to sacrifice home, job and family to go and fight, so too conscientious objectors should sacrifice their homes and jobs for their principles. Most conscientious objectors agreed.

HUMANITARIAN WORK

Conscientious objectors also worked for the Friends Ambulance Unit (FAU). Set up by Quakers at the very start of the war, the FAU aimed to give help to those suffering from war. All members were volunteers and pacifists and most of them were Quakers.

The FAU started with just 43 men; by the end of the war membership had reached well over 1,000. The first group of volunteers went to France in October 1914, where they were shocked to find rows of dreadfully wounded soldiers lying on stretchers in huge warehouses. The FAU set up field hospitals, organised ambulances and hospital trains and worked with the wounded and refugees. The FAU was widely respected. Its work helped the public to see that COs were not difficult people: they wanted to help society.

One volunteer was Corder Catchpool, a Quaker and lifelong pacifist who believed war was against the wishes of God. Like other members of the FAU, he declared he would never pick up arms and kill. He worked with the wounded in France for nearly two years, writing detailed letters about his experiences, which were later published as *On Two Fronts: Letters of a Conscientious Objector*.

When conscription was introduced, all FAU members applied for exemption from combatant duties. Because of their work they got exemption on condition they continued working with the FAU. A few members, including Corder Catchpool, were not happy about this: they would work with the FAU as volunteers but would not be forced to do so under the Military Service Act. Consequently Catchpool left the FAU and served time in prison.

> I SHALL NEVER IN MY LIFE FORGET the sight and sounds that met us… on each stretcher a wounded man – DESPERATELY WOUNDED… The air heavy with the stench of putrid flesh and thick with groans and cries…
>
> *Corder Catchpool*

HOME OFFICE SCHEME

In June 1916 the government introduced a special scheme to try and reduce the number of conscientious objectors in prison. It was called the Home Office Scheme. Conscientious objectors in prison, who had been through a court-martial, would appear before a special tribunal set up in Wormwood Scrubs. The objectors would be interviewed and, if found to be genuine, would be offered 'work of national importance', released from prison and sent to work in special work centres and camps. They would still be prisoners but would have more freedom, including the right to talk and leave the camps.

Absolutists refused to have anything to do with the government scheme and chose to remain in prison. However just over 4,000 conscientious objectors accepted the scheme, including 23 of the men who had been sentenced to death in France.

BECOMING AN ABSOLUTIST

John (Bert) Brocklesby, one of the 'Frenchmen', accepted the Home Office Scheme because he believed he would do useful work. He was sent to Dyce, where he came to believe 'the aim was to wangle us into the war machine.' He chose to return to prison to join the absolutists and later said that the Home Office Scheme turned him from an alternativist to an absolutist. Other objectors felt the same way and returned to prison.

DYCE WORK CAMP

One work camp was near the village of Dyce, just outside Aberdeen, Scotland. The first 250 men arrived in the summer; they were housed in old army tents and were put to work in the local quarry, breaking rocks. At first they were pleased to be in the fresh air and able to talk openly to each other. When autumn arrived though the conditions became atrocious. Pouring rain turned the camp into a quagmire, the tents leaked and, with nowhere to dry their clothes, the men lived and slept in constantly wet conditions. In October one CO, Walter Roberts, died from exhaustion and exposure. His death shocked his fellow objectors, some of whom decided to leave the scheme and go back to prison. It also shocked the authorities and Dyce was closed down.

'I saw young **WALTER ROBERTS** fighting a **LOSING BATTLE WITH PNEUMONIA**, brought on… by sleeping in a damp bed… he should have been carried to a proper hospital… he passed out, **A TRUE MARTYR TO THE CAUSE** of Peace and Brotherhood.'

John (Bert) Brocklesby

PRINCETOWN

One work centre was based at Dartmoor Prison. Prisoners were moved elsewhere and the prison was renamed the Princetown Work Centre. About 1,000 conscientious objectors were sent there. The work was hard: breaking rocks in the quarry, just like convicts. However, prison cells were unlocked, objectors ran their own newspapers and organised social events such as concerts, plays and lectures. After a while some went out to work for local employers.

> '… the men here are **PREPARED TO PERFORM THE WORK** provided… but protest against the penal character of the work imposed… and **DEMAND CIVIL WORK** of real importance with **FULL CIVIL RIGHTS**…'
>
> *COs' statement, Princetown*

Many local people were quite friendly and some, particularly Quakers, invited COs to their homes. However the local press and national papers such as the *Daily Mail* whipped up hatred against the objectors, accusing them of being lazy and the 'Dartmoor Do-Nothings'. As a result, some local people attacked and beat up many COs. The men published a statement saying they were not pampered. Their lives might not be as dreadful as those of soldiers in the trenches, but COs on the Home Office Scheme still had a very hard time.

The Home Office Scheme lasted 33 months. The government thought it was a success because it took so many COs out of prison. Some conscientious objectors who took the scheme felt they had compromised too much and wondered if their decision was right.

DEATHS

Appalling living and working conditions took a heavy toll. Twenty-seven conscientious objectors died and three were diagnosed as insane as a result of working on the Home Office Scheme.

'THE WORK WE DID THERE WAS WORSE THAN FUTILE… I spent ten months on the moor… the agricultural work was absolutely penal and organised on lines as for convicts… There was a hand roller, to which eight men were harnessed… I HAVE BEEN ONE OF THOSE HUMAN HORSES…'

Mark Hayler

WAR ENDS

On 11 November 1918 fighting in the First World War ended. An armistice was declared. More than 1,000 conscientious objectors were still in prison. They were not released until several months after Armistice Day.

HEARING THE NEWS

When fighting ended, conscientious objectors in prisons around Britain heard the news. Some objectors, such as John Brocklesby, Fred Murfin and Norman Gaudie, were working in a prison workshop, repairing shirts and shoes. They heard buzzers hooting all over Maidstone and knew the fighting was over.

Others were in punishment cells but they still heard cheering outside the prison walls celebrating the end of a war that cost the lives of nearly 10 million men worldwide.

WAITING

Many conscientious objectors thought they would be released immediately but this was not the case. The government and War Office wanted to release soldiers from their duties first before even beginning to think about conscientious objectors. The British public too would have been furious if 'conchies' had been released before soldiers.

A small minority of objectors protested against this situation. There was a wave of hunger and work strikes in most prisons and many of those who took part were punished severely. One objector was strapped into a straitjacket for 24 hours for going on hunger strike and was not allowed to go to the lavatory. Most though accepted their lot and just waited for the end.

> We took a pledge to **RESIST CONSCRIPTION** and the military power. **WE HAVE SURVIVED THE TEST.**
>
> *Clifford Allen*

RELEASE

By now some objectors had been in prison for well over two years. Many were weak and suffering ill health. Pressure for their release had begun in 1917 but once the fighting was over it intensified. Trade union branches, the Labour Party, Quaker organisations and influential individuals put pressure on the government to release the objectors. Even *The Times* newspaper, which was fiercely anti-'conchie', asked whether it was fair to continue punishing these men.

EARLY RELEASES

In December 1917 the first 300 conscientious objectors were released from prison. All were suffering poor health. They included Clifford Allen, who by now weighed only 8 stone, had a serious lung condition and was probably only days away from death. Several influential people had lobbied the government for their release. They included Mrs Margaret Hobhouse, whose son Stephen Hobhouse was a CO. Her book *I Appeal Unto Caesar* helped to persuade the government to release weak and dying objectors.

Finally in April 1919, six months after the guns had fallen silent, the conscientious objectors were released from prison. They were released in batches and the last did not leave prison until August 1919. In April 1919 the Home Office Scheme work camps were closed down but COs from the Non-Combatant Corps (NCC) were not released until 1920.

Interestingly when John Brocklesby and his friends were released from Maidstone Prison, ordinary prisoners clapped and cheered them for the brave men they were.

STRANGE LOGIC

When COs were finally released from prison in 1919 most were amused by a discharge notice they received from the army. As CO Wilfred Littleboy remembered: 'I have this document, "Discharged for misconduct", and printed over it in red ink that if I try to enlist again I was liable for two years' imprisonment.' Clearly the army had never quite understood that conscientious objectors were not and never would be soldiers.

DIFFICULTIES

Life was difficult for conscientious objectors after the war. Some, though not all, returned home and were shocked to find many people still hated them for having refused to fight. Those who were married often found that their wives and families were nearly destitute. Several had been abandoned by former friends.

It was hard to find work. Several objectors who applied for jobs found that banks, councils and businesses were not prepared to employ conscientious objectors, and certainly not those who had been to prison. Some job advertisements specifically stated that conscientious objectors should not apply, something that would be unlikely today when equal opportunities and human rights are so important.

Conscientious objectors also lost the right to vote. In 1917 the government debated a new Representation of the People Bill that would, when it became law in 1918, give some British women the right to vote for the very first time. Conscientious objectors, however, who had been exempted from military service or who had been court-martialled, were not allowed to vote for five years from the end of the war.

For most conscientious objectors the right to vote was not as important as finding a job and regaining their health.

Gradually most objectors, often with the help of sympathetic friends and organisations, began to find jobs and rebuild their lives. Some, such as Corder Catchpool, continued doing socially useful work with refugees and others displaced by war. Others, such as Fenner Brockway and Stephen Hobhouse, shocked by the conditions they had found in prison, devoted some years to working for prison reform.

Despite their prison records, Fenner Brockway and Clifford Allen eventually entered Parliament. Brockway became a Labour MP and both of them became Lords. Another ten COs also went on to be MPs, so proving perhaps just how socially responsible 'conchies' actually were.

INSPIRATIONAL ROLE MODELS

When war ended there was hardly a family that had not lost a father, brother, son or fiancé. People hoped that such a war would never happen again.

In Britain a new and large peace movement emerged as individuals and organisations came together to work for peace. Conscientious objectors, such as Harold Bing and Fenner Brockway, played a leading role helping to found and lead new peace organisations such as the No More War Movement and War Resisters' International. They inspired a new generation of men and women, who were powerfully influenced by the courage and determination of the men who had suffered so much and had proved it was possible for individuals to take a principled stand against a government.

KITE FLYING

A suffragette, Catherine Marshall (1880–1961), was one of many clever women who helped to keep the NCF going during the war. When Fenner Brockway was imprisoned, Catherine Marshall took over his role as secretary. On one occasion imprisoned COs smuggled a letter out to the NCF asking whether they would agree to them organising a protest strike. The NCF should signal YES by flying a red flag, or NO by flying a white flag on a tree outside the prison. Knowing she could not climb a tree, Catherine Marshall with another woman, Lydia Smith, arranged for children to fly white kites (for NO) outside the prison. The kites became stuck in the tree and the strike did not go ahead.

Despite the efforts of peace campaigners, war came again. In 1939 the Second World War broke out and lasted until 1945. Conscription – military and industrial – was introduced. Once again men, and women as well, stood as conscientious objectors and refused to be conscripted to fight and kill or have any part in the military machine. This time there were about 60,000 conscientious objectors, including 1,000 women. Most said they owed their inspiration to the conscientious objectors of the First World War.

Largely due to the courage and determination of the First World War objectors, the government took a more understanding and humane attitude in 1939–45. Although COs were ridiculed, criticised, sacked from their jobs and accused of being traitors, and some even went to prison, they were not treated as brutally as men had been in the First World War. Tribunals were fairer and COs' beliefs were more respected. The government had learned its lesson: the authorities knew that men and women who believed that war was wrong would stick to their principles.

CONSCIENTIOUS OBJECTION TODAY

The conscientious objectors of a hundred years ago still continue to inspire men and women today who believe that war is wrong and peaceful methods must be found to end conflict. During the 1960s and 1970s possibly as many as 30,000 to 40,000 young American men took a stand as war resisters or draft dodgers, refusing to fight in Vietnam. Some were imprisoned, others fled to Canada or Britain. More recently, men such as Joe Glenton and Bradley Manning have conscientiously objected to serving in Afghanistan and Iraq, and in Israel war resisters have refused to enter military service. Today also conscientious objection has extended to refusing to work in weapons factories and research. Some people have also refused to pay a percentage of their taxes as a conscientious objection to funding war and militarism. The legacy of those first 'conchies' still marches on.

> **WHAT DID WE COs ACHIEVE** in the First World War? … we proved that any decent modern government could not coerce man's conscience… we set the motion of conscientious objection really going… **WE STARTED A MOVEMENT** which means that **no war can be fought in the future without conscientious objection coming up.**
>
> *George Dutch*

COMMEMORATING COs

On 15 May each year peace activists mark International Conscientious Objectors Day. In London the Peace Pledge Union (PPU) organises a short ceremony to remember conscientious objectors who have refused to kill. The PPU funded a commemorative stone, which was unveiled in 1994.

GLOSSARY

Cad: a rude or ill-mannered man

Call up: to call for military service

Cat and mouse: the process by which objectors were released from prison, sent back into the army, and re-imprisoned after they refused orders. It took its name from the 'cat and mouse' treatment used on suffragettes, militant women who fought for the vote. Suffragettes in prison went on hunger strike. When they became very weak they were allowed out of prison. Then, like a cat playing with a mouse, the authorities re-arrested them when they were healthier and put them back into prison.

Coerce: to force

Combatant: someone who fights. A combat is a battle.

Compelled: to be forced to do something

Conchie/Conshie/CO: conscientious objector

Conscience: a personal belief in what is right or wrong

Conscription: compulsory military service. People can also be conscripted to do certain jobs in wartime. In 1940 women in Britain were conscripted for work and the armed forces.

Court-martial: a military court where people who have broken military rules are tried and sentenced

Exemption: being freed or let off from a duty

Fellowship of Reconciliation (FoR): Christian pacifist organisation founded in 1915. It still continues today.

Gospels: the teachings of Jesus Christ

Imperialism: empire building

Jehovah's Witness: a member of a Christian organisation founded in the USA in the 19th century. Jehovah's Witnesses do not recognise human governments; they believe in God's word and will not take part in wars.

Manifesto: a statement of beliefs

Military Service Act, 1916: the Act that introduced conscription into Britain in 1916

Nationalism: a powerful belief in one's own country or nation

No More War Movement (NMWM): founded in 1921 as a successor to the No-Conscription Fellowship. Its aims were to work for peace and prevent war. Fenner Brockway was its chairman.

No-Conscription Fellowship (NCF): founded in 1914 to support and bring conscientious objectors together

Non-Combatant Corps (NCC): a special non-fighting unit in the army created by the British government in 1916 as an army unit for conscientious objectors

Pacifist: a person who believes that war and violence are always wrong, no matter what the reasons for them

Patriotism: love of one's country

Peace Pledge Union (PPU): the pacifist organisation founded by pacifist Dick Sheppard in 1934. The PPU still campaigns today for a world without war.

Penal: giving out punishment

Quaker: a member of the Religious Society of Friends, a Christian group founded by George Fox in about 1650. Most members are pacifists and have a long tradition of working for peace and social justice.

Shirker: a person who tries to avoid hard work or doing something they do not want to do

Suffragettes: women who fought for the vote using dramatic methods, often involving breaking the law

Trenches: the system of parallel ditches, often built up with sandbags to offer protection from enemy fire

Volunteer: someone who offers or chooses to do something of his or her own free will

War Resisters' International: a pacifist organisation founded in Holland in 1921, it moved headquarters to London in 1923 and still exists today. Original members included First World War conscientious objectors.

INDEX